BADMINTON

By
Sir George Thomas, Bart.
All England Champion, 1921, 1922 & 1923

With Illustrations

Copyright © 2013 Read Books Ltd.
This book is copyright and may not be
reproduced or copied in any way without
the express permission of the publisher in writing

British Library Cataloguing-in-Publication Data
A catalogue record for this book is available from the
British Library

A History of Badminton

Badminton is a racquet sport played by either two opposing players (singles) or two opposing pairs (doubles). Players will take positions on opposite halves of a rectangular court divided by a net. They score points by striking a shuttlecock with their racquet so that it passes over the net and lands in their opponents half of the court – each side may only strike the shuttlecock once before it passes over the net. A rally ends once the shuttlecock has struck the floor, or if a fault has been called by either the umpire or service judge or, in their absence, the offending player, at any time during the rally.

The beginnings of badminton can be traced to the mid-1800s in British India, where it was created by British military officers stationed there. Being particularly popular in the British garrison town Poona (now **Pune**), the game also came to be known as *Poona*. Early photographs show Englishmen adding a net to the traditional English game of 'battledore and shuttlecock'. This earlier variant involved attempting to bat the shuttlecock from one player to the other as many times as possible, without allowing it to fall to the ground. Initially, balls of wool were preferred by the upper classes in windy or wet conditions, but ultimately the shuttlecock (usually made of feathers and cork) retained its popularity.

Although it is clear that Badminton House, Gloucestershire, owned by the Duke of Beaufort has given its name to the sport, it is unclear when and why the name was adopted. As early as 1860, Isaac Spratt, a London toy dealer, published a booklet, *Badminton Battledore – A New Game,* but unfortunately no copy has survived. This early use has cast doubt on the origin through expatriates in India, though it is known that it was popular there in the 1870s and that the first rules were drawn up in Poonah in 1873. Another source cites that it was in 1877 at **Karachi** in (British) India, where the first attempt was made to form a set of rules.

By 1875 however, veterans returning from India started a club in Folkestone. Until 1887, when the Bath Badminton Club standardised the rules, the sport was played in England under the system that prevailed in British India. In 1893, the Badminton Association of England published the first set of rules according to these regulations, similar to today's rules, and officially launched badminton in a house called 'Dunbar' at Six Waverley Grove, **Portsmouth**, England on September 13th of that year. They also started the *All England Open Badminton Championships*, the first badminton competition in the world, in 1899.

Badminton has since spread all over the globe. The *International Badminton Federation* was established in 1934 with Canada, Denmark, England, France, the Netherlands, Ireland, New Zealand, Scotland, and Wales as its founding members. India joined as an affiliate in 1936. Since 1992, Badminton has been an Olympic sport with five events: men's and women's singles, men's and women's doubles, and mixed doubles in which each pair consists of a man and a woman. Denmark and the Asian nations have been particularly dominant, with Denmark, China, Indonesia, South Korea and Malaysia consistently producing world-class players. At high levels of play, especially in singles, the sport demands excellent fitness, players require aerobic stamina, agility, explosive strength, speed and precision. It is also a technical sport, requiring good **motor coordination** and the development of sophisticated racquet movements. We hope that the current reader is inspired by this book to play some badminton of their own! Enjoy.

Plates 1—2

Top: BACKHAND STROKE DOWN THE LINE (J. L. RANKIN).
A DELICATE PLACING SHOT, CONTROLLED ENTIRELY BY THE ACTION OF THE WRIST.

Bottom: FOREHAND STROKE DOWN THE LINE (J. L. RANKIN).
THE DIRECTION OF THE STROKE HAS BEEN GOVERNED BY LETTING THE WRIST GIVE BACK, AT THE MOMENT OF IMPACT, IN RELATION TO THE ARM.

LIST OF CONTENTS

CHAP.		PAGE
1.	History of the Game	9
2.	General Principles of Stroke Play	12
3.	Individual Strokes	18
4.	Service and Return of Service	28
5.	Singles	31
6.	Doubles	37
7.	The Laws of Badminton	45

LIST OF PLATES

PLATE

1. BACKHAND STROKE DOWN THE LINE (J. L. RANKIN) *Frontispiece*
2. FOREHAND STROKE DOWN THE LINE (J. L. RANKIN) ,,

FACING PAGE

3. FOREHAND DROP-SHOT (R. C. F. NICHOLS) . . . 25
4. BACKHAND CROSS-COURT DROP-SHOT (D. C. HUME) . 25
5. WAITING FOR THE SERVICE (R. M. WHITE) . . . 30
6. HIGH BACKHAND LOB (R. C. F. NICHOLS) . . . 35
7. FINISH OF SMASH (R. M. WHITE) 35

CHAPTER ONE

HISTORY OF THE GAME

TO a rainy day, and a house-party seeking some new diversion, belongs the honour of evolving Badminton from the ancient child's pastime of battledore and shuttlecock. One of the party (whose name unfortunately remains shrouded in obscurity), struck by a bright idea, stretched a cord across the hall, commandeered the children's toys—and Badminton, in its most primitive form, came into being. So much did it prove to the taste of the party that it became an established amusement of that particular house and so derived its name—from Badminton, the famous country seat in Gloucestershire. That at any rate is generally believed to be the origin of the game; and the date some sixty-five to seventy years ago.

From this starting-point the game, though as yet without any very definite rules, found its way to other places—among them India. And there the first attempts to frame a regular code were made. These were printed in 1877 at Karachi, where it is known the game had already been played for half a dozen years or so; though for lack of anything in the nature of a governing body, such a code could have only local authority. It became, however, the basis of the rules adopted when an Association was eventually formed, and was responsible for a very peculiar feature which survived for many years. The hall in which the game was played at Karachi was not much wider than the court itself, and had doors opening inwards at the centre. To allow for these, the side-lines were bent inwards between the short service-lines and the net, the width at the net being thus several feet less than that of the greater part of the court. This curious formation—known as the 'hour-glass' court—became an integral point of the game, and was not abolished until 1901.

While India certainly played the chief part in the early development of the game, it had already gained a footing in other quarters of the globe. The New York club, for example, celebrated its jubilee several years ago. But the dimensions of the court were a matter of local convenience, and varied greatly. Every sort of implement, too, was used. Vellum-covered rackets held the field in India for many years; and I remember, as a small boy, seeing the game played in a large room in our house in Constantinople with tennis rackets and enormous shuttlecocks at least four times the bulk of the present-day article.

Uniformity in essentials became practical politics in 1893, with the formation in England of the Badminton Association. The prime movers were players returned from India, which explains the adoption of the 'hour-glass' court; but from that date England took, and has ever since held, the lead in the development of the game. At its inception, the Association comprised only about a dozen clubs; and progress for the first few years was slow. The All England Championships were not instituted until 1899, and the first meeting was a very small affair, played through in one day! But it certainly gave the game a considerable fillip, and from that date headway was made much more rapidly. The Irish Badminton Union was the next important organization to come into being, and started its own championships in 1902, Scotland following suit in 1907. During the previous year or two there had been a marked development of tournament play throughout England, many of the most important tournaments in the country dating from that period.

The annual matches between England and Ireland were started in 1903. Scotland entered the arena in 1910—when its series of matches against Ireland was initiated—but did not play England until 1922. Wales started against Ireland and Scotland in 1929, and against England in 1932, so there is now a complete list of annual fixtures between the four home countries.

Very important events in the International development of the game were the visits of a team from England to Canada in 1925 and 1930. The game has to-day a tremendous following in Canada, which seems likely to provide the strongest opposition to our home players during the next few years. There is also a very large and flourishing Association in Australia. Nearer home, Denmark and Holland have taken up the game very keenly, and other continental nations show signs of following suit, though the movement there is still in its infancy.

Few people not directly concerned realize the extent to which Badminton is played at home to-day. In England alone there are nearly a thousand affiliated clubs, and six hundred in Ireland, Scotland and Wales ; in addition, there are a legion of small clubs not yet affiliated.

An International Federation has been formed which comprises Canada, Denmark, England, France, Holland, India, Ireland, New Zealand, Scotland and Wales.

CHAPTER TWO

GENERAL PRINCIPLES OF STROKE PLAY

[*Note.*—*In this and the chapter on individual strokes I deal with the actions of a right-handed player. In the case of a left-handed player, the position of the feet, and so forth, must of course be reversed.*]

BEFORE considering in detail the various strokes at a player's command, it is as well to point out certain general principles which should govern all his actions. These principles should be kept continually in mind when particular strokes are being considered in the next chapter. It is true that they have a more important bearing on some strokes—those especially which require a good deal of force for their proper execution—than on others. But they are of value all the time ; fundamentals without which no player can develop any real mastery over the shuttlecock.

As in all kindred games, correct stroke production depends as much on footwork as on manipulation of the racket. Feet wrongly placed destroy the whole rhythm of a stroke, spoiling the poise of the body and making it impossible to throw the weight into the balance, where required, at exactly the right moment. Moreover, any stroke finishing with the weight wrongly disposed seriously impairs the ability to move instantaneously in any direction.

The position of the feet is particularly important in backhand strokes. In *every* stroke played on the backhand, the right foot should be in advance of the left, and to some extent across it. In no other position can the arm be allowed free play on the left side of the body. The extent to which the right foot should be brought across towards the left side-line depends on the position of the shuttlecock at the moment of impact. If the striker can take it early, that is to say at a point decidedly nearer to the net than he is himself, it is sufficient to have the right foot somewhere in front of the other. But the later the shuttlecock is taken, the farther must the right foot be carried round; until, in cases where the shuttlecock has actually passed the striker, it is between the other foot and the base-line, though still in advance of the left foot in relation to the direction in which the body is facing. This position of the feet in backhand strokes is not only necessary from the point of view, sufficiently obvious, of giving the arm room in which to swing; but is also essential to control of balance whenever the weight of the body has to be brought into play.

For forehand strokes the converse is only partially true. Here the poise of the body is the main, if not the only, consideration, since the arm has naturally free scope. Therefore, though the left foot should usually be somewhat in advance, it should not, as a general rule, be brought across. Doing so, to any pronounced extent, tends to impede instead of to free the arm. There are, of course, occasions when, in running for the shuttlecock, it is impossible to reach it at all, except with the left foot well over towards the right side-line; and forehand strokes can be played quite well in that position—but as a matter of necessity, not of choice. In the majority of cases, the player can so order his movement, by varying the length of his steps, that his final stride leaves him with his feet in the most suitable position.

In forehand strokes played overhead, the position of the feet is far more important than in the case of those played underhand. In the latter, although the body should be properly poised, the actual force of the stroke depends almost entirely—except, perhaps, in a very powerful drive—on the movement of the arm and wrist. In overhead strokes, however, the weight of the body, properly used, is a vital factor. Even when the stroke actually played does not require much force, the option of throwing the full weight into it, if required, should be reserved; so that the action, up to the very moment of impact, may be precisely the same whatever the intention behind it. In these strokes, therefore, the advanced position of the left foot is of particular importance.

With the feet correctly placed, it is a simple matter to use the weight of the body as far as may be necessary. At the commencement of the stroke, the weight should be supported mainly by the foot farther from the net; being then transferred, at the precise moment of impact, to the other foot. This is true of *all* strokes, even when the minimum of force is required; for in no other way can the striker have his balance properly under control, and the ability to move instantaneously in any direction, directly the stroke is completed, assured. The greater the force required, the more emphatically should the transfer of weight be effected; and in the case of certain strokes, such as a full-blooded smash, or a backhand clearing stroke taken low and near the base-line, the forward swing of the body should be very pronounced indeed.

Coming now to the part played in stroke production by hand and arm, the first thing to consider is the grip. With very slight variations, most strong players use what may be called the normal grip. In this, the knuckles at the base of the fingers lie diagonally across one of the facets of the handle in the same plane as the face of the racket (see Plate 1). This is, I am sure, much the most suitable and natural grip for the great majority of strokes, though the exact position of fingers and thumb may be modified to suit the size of the player's hand, and the size and shape of the handle he uses. Personally, I always keep the end portion of my thumb turned downwards, and use exactly the same grip for practically all forehand and backhand strokes. But many players—including some of the greatest—point the thumb up the handle for backhand strokes; a position which, they say, helps to control direction. Though I never found that so myself, the point is one on which a player should follow the method which comes naturally to him. Some players also turn the handle slightly for backhand strokes; but that, I consider, is definitely wrong. The practice is, of course, a very general one among lawn-tennis players; but the considerations which recommend it in that game do not apply in Badminton, since there is no question of imparting top-spin and the trajectory of a drive is so much higher.

Although the normal grip is best for most purposes, there is an alternative very suitable for certain strokes. In this, the racket is given about a quarter-turn, so that the base knuckles of the fingers are at the side of that facet of the handle across which they lie in the normal position. The front view of this grip is shown in Plate 2. This grip is very convenient for quick movement of the racket more or less in front of the striker's face, and is used largely by players who specialize at the net in back-and-front doubles. But it is definitely inferior for the majority of strokes played from the back of

GENERAL PRINCIPLES OF STROKE PLAY 15

the court; and those players who use it exclusively are often hampered by it. What it comes to is this: the normal grip is good for all purposes; the alternative only for special strokes; and those who use it near the net should train themselves to change to the normal position when farther back in court.

Now for the actual striking of the shuttlecock—the action of the arm and wrist. The first consideration is to time matters so that the racket connects with the shuttlecock at the exact point where its flight can be most effectively controlled in regard to both pace and direction. This will usually be accomplished by having the arm at practically full stretch at the moment of impact. Hitting with a bent elbow wastes power. This applies only to the actual moment of impact. During the preliminary swing the elbow should be freely bent and quite loose. While the straightening of the arm is usually a gradual process, the elbow should remain loose up to the moment of impact, becoming taut exactly when the shuttlecock is struck. Correct timing in this respect is a great aid to power. When defending at close quarters, taking shots off the body for example, it will often be impossible to use a straight arm; but even then the shuttlecock should be taken as far away as possible; and even when there is no time to move the feet, a good deal of extra freedom can be given to the arm by swaying the body away from the line of flight of the shuttlecock. In certain delicately played strokes, a slightly bent elbow is no disadvantage. But Badminton is a game in which it is of vital consequence to conceal one's intention; and precisely the same action should be used, and the same position assumed, whether the intention is to hit hard or not.

This last point is of great importance in connection with the preliminary swing of the racket, which should be sufficiently vigorous to allow of the shuttlecock being struck with the greatest force suitable to the occasion, even though something quite different be intended. The swing itself should be free and smooth, with no break between the backward and forward movements.

At the moment of impact—or rather at the least possible fraction of a second earlier—the wrist should take control of the stroke. It may already have come into action of a sort in helping to bring the head of the racket to the desired position; but its real function is to govern direction, and as far as possible pace, when the shuttlecock is being actually struck.

This is the basis of all those deceptive strokes which are such a fascinating feature of Badminton. By a turn of the wrist at the last moment, the shuttlecock can be sent in a direction entirely different from that which would naturally follow from the general swing of the arm; and the more completely any such change of direction is worked by the wrist, without any modification of the movement of the arm, the better will be the effect. The angle of elevation, as well as the lateral direction of a stroke, should be controlled in this way. While this action of the wrist should be timed to take effect as late as possible, it must come into play just before the actual moment of impact; otherwise the shuttlecock will not be cleanly hit.

As far as pace is concerned, *extreme* variations cannot be produced by the wrist alone; and in such cases the swing of the arm must be either quickened or retarded to help towards the desired effect. When necessary, this should be done as late as possible (so as to conceal the intention), though not so late as to produce a jerky movement. But the wrist can, unaided, regulate the pace of the stroke to a surprising extent; and whenever possible it should be left to do so; since, being the last agent to come into play, it best serves that never-to-be-neglected purpose of concealing the nature of the intended stroke.

It is quite as important to be able to check as to increase the pace of a stroke by means of the wrist. This is done by relaxing the muscles and letting the wrist and hand loiter, so to speak, in comparison with the rest of the arm; by this means it is possible to strike the shuttlecock very gently indeed, though the arm itself is still moving at considerable speed. This artifice, at any rate in the frequency and extent of its application, is something quite peculiar to Badminton; and full command of it is absolutely essential to any player who aspires to real proficiency. Increase of speed by means of the wrist is, of course, common to all kindred games, and is obtained by a flick of the wrist and a tightening of the muscles, which, to produce the proper effect, must be very accurately timed.

Every correctly executed stroke—even the most delicate of drop-shots—will finish with the appropriate follow-through; except when it is deliberately checked, as in the case of a smash played from within striking distance of the net. The more forceful the stroke, the more pronounced should be the follow-through. But it should be kept in mind that the right amount of follow-through is the result of correct methods, not a contributory factor. Regarded in that light, it may afford valuable indication of certain faults in execution. Whenever an attempt to hit hard results in an inadequate or jerky follow-through it is an almost certain sign of one of two mistakes. The striker has either misjudged his distance from the shuttlecock or has had his feet wrongly placed. As he corrects either of these faults he will find that the follow-through becomes automatically more free and smooth; and its improvement, so long as it is the natural consequence of some change in his earlier movements, will show him that he is working on the right lines. But only when it *is* the natural consequence. His stroke will not be in the least improved by the artificial addition of extra follow-through after the crucial moment of impact.

I have already pointed out the necessity of playing strokes in such a way as to conceal the intention as long as possible. The importance of this cannot be over-estimated. A stroke which, if unanticipated by the opponent, may be highly effective, may be worse than useless if he can tell it is coming. So it is absolutely essential to be able to play widely different strokes without any variation in the preliminary action. But that is only the first stage in the art of keeping the opponent guessing. Once that has been mastered, actual feinting—the attempt to convey false information—should be assiduously cultivated. To do this effectively is far from easy; and no golden rule for its performance can be laid down, for the very reason that, if worked by rule, it would be of no value against any intelligent opponent. But even the most alert adversary may be tricked now and again—by some subtly conveyed suggestion—into moving the wrong way; which is, of course, far more effective than merely keeping him as long as possible from moving in the right direction.

CHAPTER THREE

INDIVIDUAL STROKES

OF the various strokes in the game, a really powerful smash is the most potent. It is the chief weapon of aggression and the most frequent means of pressing home an advantage. In smashing, severity is, of course, the first essential; and severity depends, not only on the amount of force used, but even more on the precise way in which that force is applied. The weight of the body *must* be thrown into the scale at exactly the right moment; and the wrist *must* be used to give that extra sting which is the hall-mark of an effective smash. To make the transference of weight fully effective, the body should be bent back to some extent at the commencement of the stroke, so that when it is thrown forward it has extra momentum; but the shuttlecock should not be struck until the body is well started on its forward movement. The exact point at which it should be struck varies slightly with the action of individual players; but as a rough guide it may be given as somewhere vertically above the feet, and, of course, as high as possible. Smashing with the arm not fully extended is a common fault which wastes a great deal of power.

Some first-class players smash from a point above the right shoulder; others (the majority, I think) bring the racket up behind the head and smash from over the left shoulder. Either method is perfectly good, and a player may safely adopt, for general use, whichever comes most naturally to him. But he should also be able to resort to the alternative method on occasion—when, for example, he has not enough time to get properly under the shuttlecock for the position he prefers. Anyone who can only smash in one position will find his opportunities of doing so greatly restricted by an opponent who plays with his head.

If there *is* anything to choose between the two methods, preference goes, I think, to smashing from above the left shoulder—or round the head, as it is commonly described. Players who use this action have possibly a slightly greater facility in turning the smash in any direction, and in concealing the direction until the shuttlecock leaves the racket. And this is hardly less important than severity. Except in the case of a 'sitter', even the most ferocious smash loses a great deal of its effect if its direction can be foreseen. Only when a player has equal facility in smashing straight down or across the court in either direction, without any change of preliminary action, can he be said to have attained real mastery over the stroke.

When smashing with full force, there will naturally be a very pronounced follow-through—of body, arm and racket. Played from a correct position, this leaves the player sufficiently well balanced for quick movement, especially in a forward direction; played, however, from an unsound position—especially with regard to the feet—the result is a loss of balance which leaves the striker momentarily helpless, should his smash be returned with a quick stroke at some awkward angle. So that careless methods when smashing not only impair the stroke itself, but are also a source of actual danger to the striker.

When smashing from anywhere within reach of the net, the follow-through of the racket must be checked sufficiently to avoid any risk of touching the net. This is done by a sharp upward jerk of the wrist immediately after impact with the shuttlecock. It must, on occasion, be a very abrupt movement indeed; but, properly executed, it enables the shuttlecock to be struck really hard, from within a few inches of the net, without disaster. When a stroke of this nature is played on the backhand, it is also useful to turn the body away from the net at the critical moment.

The backhand smash, in general, is only a colourless imitation of the forehand variety. From any point fairly near the net, however, it can be a very snappy and effective weapon. Its limitations are due to the fact that it is quite impossible to use the weight of the body in the same way as in the smash proper; so that pace depends on the action of arm and wrist only. Consequently, it can never approach the forehand smash in severity. There are, it is true, occasions when the backhand smash can be usefully employed from quite a long way back in court; but in such cases its value depends on the placing, not on the pace of the shot. Almost invariably, it is better to move sideways and secure position for playing the stroke with a forehand action.

As a general rule, a smash should be brought down at as steep an angle as possible. Deep smashing to the base-line is sometimes desirable; but in nine cases out of ten the shorter the smash, the greater will be its effect. This, once more, is the business of the wrist, and depends on the accurate timing of the downward flick.

While the smash is the spearhead of attack, the lob is the main bulwark of defence, though its use is by no means confined to defensive work; and its characteristics differ widely, according as the idea behind it is offensive or defensive. Treating it first as a means of defence, the main considerations are length and height. Poor length in defensive lobbing is a fatal error against an opponent with a useful smash. That is such an obvious truism that it would seem unnecessary to rub it in; yet it is quite the commonest fault in the game, even among players of a considerable degree of skill. A defensive lob should be considered of definitely bad length if it would fall as much as 2 feet short of the base-line, and every inch beyond that is a matter of real importance. Some first-class players develop almost uncanny accuracy in this direction, and can put up lob after lob which would fall not more than 2 or 3 inches inside the line. The beginner will be well advised to lob too far rather than not far enough. He will find it much easier to tone down this form of error than to correct the opposite tendency.

Though not of such obvious importance as length, height is also of value in defensive lobbing. It serves two purposes. In the first place, it affords valuable time during which a player who has been driven out of position can return to his base; and in the second place, the shuttlecock will be falling almost vertically before coming within reach of the opponent, and will on that account be all the more difficult to smash. Some strong players carry the principle of hitting high too far, in my opinion; overdone, it is merely a waste of time and energy; but within reasonable limits its importance cannot be gainsaid.

The importance of varying the direction of defensive lobs is often overlooked. Most players have a tendency to play these strokes almost exclusively straight down the court.

INDIVIDUAL STROKES

That is a great mistake. It is quite as important to cultivate variety in defensive as in attacking measures. In lobbing across the court, however, it is more than ever important to use sufficient height, owing to the extra danger of interception by the opponent.

The lob used as an attacking weapon is based on entirely different principles. Here, the idea is to take advantage of some difficulty in the opponent's position by directing the shuttlecock to the particular point at the back of the court towards which he will find it hardest to move. Saving of time becomes, therefore, the main consideration, and the shuttlecock should be kept as low as possible—consistent, naturally, with avoidance of any chance of interception. Length, also, becomes a minor virtue, its sacrifice often being more than compensated for by the time saved through the shorter distance the shuttlecock has to travel; this saving of time, though infinitesimal, may make all the difference in taking advantage of an opponent's momentary loss of mobility.

The only lobs which present any mechanical difficulty are those played on the backhand from somewhere in the region of the base-line, whether high in the air or near the ground. In these cases it is not easy to develop the very considerable degree of power necessary for a good-length stroke. In a backhand lob played overhead, the weight of the body hardly comes into play at all; the work must be done by the wrist and arm, and only by perfect timing can the requisite force be obtained. The ordinary principles of backhand play should be accentuated, the right foot being carried well across (considerably nearer than the other foot to the left side-line) and the body turned away from the net. Distance from the shuttlecock must be very accurately gauged, so that impact occurs when the upward swing of the arm has gained its maximum speed and with the arm itself, of course, at full stretch; and the flick of the wrist at the crucial moment must be very free. Properly played, there is no other stroke in the game in which so much power is developed with so little apparent effort; but there is also no other stroke in which so much energy is wasted by imperfect timing and footwork.

The backhand lob from far back in court and near the ground is very different. Here, the swing of the body is of the greatest service. To use it to the fullest advantage, the feet should be farther apart than for other strokes; therefore, in the preliminary run—this stroke is one there should never be any need to play unless one has had to run some distance—the striker should order his steps so that the last one, bringing him into position, is a long stride with the right foot. In such a position the weight can be thrown violently, yet quite naturally, into the stroke; and is of service not only in the stroke itself, but also in preparation for immediate movement back to a more central position in court. The arm and wrist must also, of course, play their allotted part freely and vigorously; but the body swing is the factor on which to concentrate.

This particular lob is among the most difficult strokes in the game; but is an absolutely essential part of every player's equipment; though in match play the situations calling for it should be avoided as far as possible, even by the most expert. When the shuttlecock can be reached in time to take it while still fairly high, it is usually best to do so, even though it may call for a little extra effort in getting quickly into position. Apart from any difficulty in the stroke itself, the player who has been forced to make his stroke from this position is not so well placed for future eventualities as if he had intercepted the shuttlecock at some earlier stage. This is one of the many situations in which an apparent saving of energy is really false economy. But there are inevitably many occasions, especially in singles and in back-and-front doubles, when the position cannot be avoided; and the stroke should therefore be tackled assiduously in practice.

Forehand lobs call for little comment, the necessary force coming quite naturally from a normal swing. The sole difficulty lies in keeping the accurate length without which these strokes, so far from playing for safety, simply ask for trouble. That only comes from practice. Overhead, the whole preliminary action should be precisely the same as in smashing; but, at the moment of striking, the weight is thrown straight forward instead of forward and downward, and the downward flick of the wrist is omitted.

To most players, I think, drop-shots are the most fascinating strokes in Badminton, just as they are its most distinctive feature. Other games—lawn tennis and squash for example—have their own drop-shots; but only for occasional use. In Badminton, they are among the most frequently used strokes, and play a very important rôle in tactics. Their variety is innumerable, and they range from strokes in which the shuttlecock travels forward no more than an inch or two to those played from any position on the base-line.

Drop-shots may be divided roughly into two classes. First, those in which the object is to make the shuttlecock fall as vertically as possible as soon as it has crossed the net; the idea here is to keep the shuttlecock so close to the net as to make its return a matter of actual difficulty for the opponent, or at least to give him the smallest possible latitude in the nature of his reply. In the second class the object is to skim the net as closely as possible without, however, bringing the shuttlecock down particularly quickly on the other side; just with the general idea of making the opponent hit upwards. When played at any considerable distance from the net, these two classes of drop-shot become entirely different. In the first case, the shuttlecock must travel at a relatively high elevation for the greater part of its flight, and must not begin to drop until within quite a short distance of the net. This is very marked in the case of an overhead drop-shot (of this type) from the base-line, in which the shuttlecock may travel almost horizontally until nearing the end of its flight, then dropping very abruptly from a considerable height; while an underhand drop-shot of this nature must be lifted well above the level of the net and also only start to drop at the last moment. This sort of stroke calls for the utmost accuracy —and its use should be reserved for suitable occasions—or it will be open to severe punishment; the margin between a perfect shot and one which can be killed by the opponent being frequently a matter of inches.

The other type of drop-shot, in which the vertical fall is not aimed at, is not nearly so dangerous in most circumstances. Here, in overhead strokes, the shuttlecock should be travelling downwards throughout its course; and in underhand strokes it should be lifted no more than will enable it to clear the net. These shots, if allowed to fall, would often pass several feet beyond the net, and yet be perfectly good drop-shots from the point of view of the effect aimed at. Though, in general, not presenting the same difficulty of return as those drop-shots which hug the net, they can be made to travel appreciably faster; and so may be the more effective weapon against an opponent who is out of position. Another point to remember is that a shot which falls very near the net, is quite likely to come back still closer, if the opponent plays an accurate drop-shot in reply; so that its very excellence may possibly be turned to the disadvantage of the striker. Not that he should be deterred from attempting to drop as closely as possible at any suitable moment.

In all drop-shots the two most important factors are firm control and concealment of the intention. However delicate the stroke may be, however slight the actual force required, that degree of force should be applied smoothly and firmly. Failure in this respect is the most frequent cause of inaccuracy in this kind of stroke. The attempt to hit very softly is allowed to degenerate into a sort of shuffle which is fatal to control. Even in those extreme cases where it seems necessary to do no more than intercept the shuttlecock in its flight and let it rebound, there will always be some degree of control to be applied by the wrist; and the more firmly it is applied, the better will be the result.

Concealment of intention is absolutely vital in drop-shots, the great majority of which depend for their effect on the element of surprise. Of course, it is only now and again that even the most cleverly disguised stroke will catch an alert opponent really unprepared; but he must at least be prevented from knowing what is intended. The preliminary motions, therefore, should be precisely the same as those for other strokes, and this applies to the positioning of the feet as much as to the swing of the racket. The force required being so small, it is quite possible—even easy—to play accurate drop-shots with the body faultily balanced; but the mere fact of their being played in such a way gives the opponent a useful clue as to what to expect.

As a general rule, it is much easier to check than to increase the pace of a stroke at the last moment; and the more pronounced the variation in pace, the truer this becomes. It is relatively easy to play a drop-shot after swinging as though for a smash, but impossible to play an effective smash without the necessary swing. Disguise of pace must, therefore, usually be based on an initial suggestion of hard hitting. It is, then, impossible to over-emphasize the necessity of playing drop-shots as though some harder stroke were intended. Neglect of this precaution naturally increases in danger with distance from the net. From near the net, a readily anticipated drop-shot—while losing much of its value—may still be comparatively safe; from the back of the court—giving the opponent, as it does, so much time for getting into position—it will, unless extraordinarily accurate, offer an easy opening.

Plates 3—4

Top: FOREHAND DROP-SHOT (R. C. F. NICHOLS).
IN SPITE OF THE SMALL DEGREE OF FORCE REQUIRED, THE ACTION IS AS FIRM AND RHYTHMIC AS IN THE MORE SEVERE STROKES.

Bottom: BACKHAND CROSS-COURT DROP-SHOT (D. C. HUME).
THE WRIST IS TURNED WELL BACK, SENDING THE SHUTTLECOCK IN THE OPPOSITE DIRECTION FROM THAT TO WHICH THE PLAYER IS FACING.

As an example, consider the case of a player compelled to take the shuttlecock near the ground in his backhand base-line corner. His safest stroke, provided he has the necessary power at command, will be a high lob to the opposite base-line; but a drop-shot, either straight down the line or across the court, will be a most useful variant, and may even open the way to attack. But should he neglect—or by reason of faulty footwork be unable—to take a full preliminary swing, his opponent, realizing that a good-length lob has become impossible, will naturally take a step or two forward in readiness to pounce on the almost inevitable drop-shot.

The better the intention has been disguised, the harder will it be to play the actual stroke with the requisite smoothness and firmness; for the natural tendency, when reducing pace drastically, is to pull up with a jerk. This must be carefully avoided; and however suddenly the force of the blow is cut off, the shuttlecock must be stroked rather than jabbed. This firm control of every species of stroke is the secret of that elusive but invaluable quality known as 'touch'.

The direction of a drop-shot should be concealed as carefully as its general nature. By means of the wrist it can be turned in any direction, from any part of the court, and in reply to any stroke; even when returning the most powerful smash, a drop-shot can be angled with perfect accuracy. The more completely the wrist governs direction, the more effective will be its concealment. In extreme cases, the shuttlecock is turned from its natural path at an angle which, to the uninitiated, looks almost miraculous. The more elaborate drop-shots are naturally difficult of execution; and even the finest players use them only occasionally when circumstances make the risk worth while. But drop-shots in general can be played with extreme certainty; and no ambitious player should be satisfied until he can control them effectively from any part of the court.

The only other classes of stroke calling for special consideration are the push-shot and the drive. The push-shot is a most valuable weapon of aggression anywhere near the net, when the shuttlecock can be taken a little above the level of the net without being in position for a smash. The stroke is played more or less directly in front of the face, and with a forehand—*not* a backhand—action. This is one of the strokes in which the alternative grip illustrated in Plate 3 may be conveniently used; and the knees should be bent sufficiently to bring the face down to the level of the shuttlecock. As there can be practically no preliminary swing in such a position, the pace depends entirely on the forearm and wrist; so although plenty of snap can be imparted there can be no great severity. Direction is, therefore, of supreme importance; and this particular stroke is usually most effective when directed straight at the opponent if—as is almost always the case when the occasion for it arises—he is anywhere near the net. Somewhere in the neighbourhood of the right shoulder is usually as vulnerable a spot as any. The absence of swing in this stroke allows it to be converted very easily into a drop-shot at the last moment; and as there is a natural tendency to give back a step when threatened with a push-shot at close quarters, the alternative drop-shop may quite possibly catch an opponent on the wrong foot.

Although most experts exploit the drive to good purpose, it is, for some obscure reason, almost entirely neglected by weaker players. Yet—although the occasions proper to its use are somewhat limited—it is far more effective at the right moment than any alternative. In many situations, with the opponent out of position, it is the only shot quick enough to be an outright winner. For its success, it depends on low trajectory and extreme pace. Occasionally, it may score by virtue of surprise. But normally, when played as a potential winner, it is intended to seize a definite opening as quickly as possible. In such a case, no desire to conceal the intention should be allowed to detract in the smallest degree from the speed of the stroke. Given sufficient speed, the opponent may be unable to arrive in time, however certainly he knows what is coming. To this end, everything that makes for pace must be brought into play —footwork, correct timing and so forth. But the dominating factor is the very full sweep of the arm, which is here of more importance than any action of the wrist. Unless the follow-through is very marked, the stroke cannot have been properly executed. The drive can be played equally well on either side; if anything, greater pace can be obtained on the backhand, as the full sweep of the arm harmonizes more naturally with the swing of the body on that side. There are, of course, plenty of situations in which the drive is played merely as an incident in the rally, not as an attempt at a winning stroke; even here, as much pace as can conveniently be introduced is desirable— though not to the extent of making the intention unduly obvious.

One last word on stroke play. In spite of the enormous influence of the wrist, this is only used for the purposes of con-

INDIVIDUAL STROKES

trolling pace and direction. There is in Badminton nothing equivalent to putting ' work ' on the ball, as in so many games. The shuttlecock does actually spin in the air, owing to the angle at which the feathers are set. But owing to its shape it can be invested with neither top-spin nor back-spin. It is just possible, by cutting tremendously hard, to impart a slight swerve ; but not enough to be of the smallest value. The *action* of cutting may occasionally be usefully employed ; but only to disguise direction, or to lessen the force of the actual blow. However much the wrist may be turned during the performance of a stroke, the racket should, in almost every case, meet the shuttlecock with an ' open ' face.

CHAPTER FOUR

SERVICE AND RETURN OF SERVICE

BADMINTON is the only game of its type in which the server starts at a disadvantage ; for he is compelled by the rules to serve underhand. And as he can only score when serving, any weakness in this respect may throw away the fruits of much good play in the rallies. Services fall into three categories—short services which just skim the net and fall as little beyond the short service-line as possible, deep lobs, and low services to the junction of the centre and long service lines, which are commonly described as drives though lacking the characteristic pace of those strokes. In all these the server should cut matters as fine as possible ; the short service *must* only just clear the net and commence to drop as soon as it is over ; the lob *must* be of really good length ; the drive service *must* be so angled as to come within the opponent's reach as late as possible. It is far better to serve an occasional fault than to put up a succession of weak services that invite punishment. There is, however, no excuse for serving frequent faults —though this is a sin surprisingly prevalent even among first-class performers. Anyone with real control over the shuttlecock should be able to serve very close to the mark with only an occasional error.

Next to accuracy, variety is the server's best resource. Even a perfect short service is not really safe if the opponent can gamble on it. He must, therefore, be kept guessing. Few players, I think, use the drive service often enough. Though possibly the most dangerous of the three types, it is the one most likely to enable the server to seize the attack. Served from the right-hand court it is especially dangerous against a player who smashes round his head, as this form of smash can be played at a comparatively low elevation. But even this danger may sometimes be turned to the server's advantage ;

as it may present an opening for a quick backhand drop across court (towards the left) which may take effect—the whole business happening so quickly—before the opponent has fully recovered from his smash.

Not only should the various types of service be mixed judiciously, but the direction of lobs and short services should also be varied. In this, however, thought must be given to any particular characteristics of the receiver. The direction of a lob service should *generally* be governed by consideration of the type of smash the receiver favours—to the left if he prefers to smash from over his right shoulder, and vice versa. But not *always*. The lob he is not expecting will often be the more effective, even though actually better suited to his style. Many players, too, are far better at rushing a short service that comes more or less straight across the net than one at an acute angle ; and where that holds good, advantage should naturally be taken of the relative weakness.

In the actual delivery of the service there are a few points to be noticed, in addition to the ordinary principles of stroke production. In holding the shuttlecock, the fingers should avoid the string which binds the lower part of the feathers. This occasionally becomes sticky and, if it clings to the fingers ever so slightly when released, will tend to inaccuracy. Most good players wait to strike until the shuttlecock is at a considerable distance from the hand ; but a few bring the head of the racket very near the left hand and strike directly the feathers are released. This latter method helps control in the case of a short service, but impairs it for other services ; so is, in my opinion, inferior on general grounds. It would, of course, be futile to adopt one method of delivery for short services and another for lobs or drives, as that would at once give away the intention.

Equally, the position in court assumed by the server should be quite independent of the particular service he intends to deliver. This is not to suggest that he should always serve from the same spot. A change in this, as in other directions, may sometimes be advisable. But such a change should not be preliminary to any particular form of service. In singles, the most favourable position for the server is, naturally, somewhere near the centre of the court. In doubles, it depends a good deal on the formation adopted by the server and his partner. Where strict back-and-front tactics are followed, serving from somewhere near the centre-line is obviously most suitable. But serving from near the side-line gives command of a much wider angle ; an important consideration—especially for the drive service.

Much poor serving is a matter of nerves. This is particularly true in regard to short services. The server has to perform one of the most critical actions in the game, in cold blood, and with an opponent, distant only a few feet from the net, waiting—in some such intimidating attitude as that illustrated in Plate 5—to pounce on the least error. It is not surprising if, when things are not going too well, his confidence is shaken. The only real remedy for this is mental—the exercise of will-power. But it will sometimes be found helpful, as a steadying influence, to serve with more than usual deliberation ; though not, of course, to the point of baulking the opponent.

The receiver of service should aim at rubbing in the advantage of his position by dealing drastically with the slightest looseness, and should go all out for a winner at the least justification. If he can make any but the most accurate service unsafe, he may, apart from any question of destroying the server's *moral*, induce him to attempt super-accuracy in aiming at his mark, and so lead to an increased number of faults. This object will be best served by assuming a more or less crouching attitude, when waiting for the service, as near the net as possible, and with the racket held well in advance of the body. In doubles a normally active man can wait close up to the short service-line, and yet be able to get back in ample time to deal properly with a lob. From this position he should be able to punish even a slightly weak short service, and have a reasonable chance of rushing a proportion of quite good ones. Anxiety to rush a short service should not, however, lead him into the error (so often committed) of trying to do so when the shuttlecock has dropped below the level of the tape before he reaches it. If he has started to rush such a service, his best plan, on finding himself a fraction of a second too late for his purpose, is to convert his intended push-stroke into a drop. In singles, with the extra depth of court at the server's command, the receiver cannot afford to wait so near the short service-line without sacrificing to some extent the ability of dealing as he wishes with a good-length lob. He will give away less by surrendering some of his chance of rushing a short service than by permitting a lob to be too safe. So he should drop back a little, the degree to which that is necessary depending on the measure of his own activity.

WAITING FOR THE SERVICE (R. M. WHITE). Plate 5

THE PLAYER IS EQUALLY READY FOR INSTANTANEOUS MOVEMENT EITHER FORWARD, TO POUNCE ON A SHORT SERVICE, OR BACKWARD FOR A LOB.

CHAPTER FIVE

SINGLES

STRONG players may be divided roughly into two schools : those who attack actively as much as possible, and those who manœuvre for an opening on more defensive lines, with safety as the first consideration. No really strong player is purely defensive. But a great deal can be accomplished by safety-first methods ; and he who hits the large majority of his shots high and deep to the base-line, mingling them with some well-judged drop-shots but seldom smashing unless he has a good chance of killing outright, is a difficult man to score off ; provided he is himself good at returning smashes and keeps an impeccable length. But while giving away little, he will not gain much ; and when two of this type meet the game becomes simply a war of attrition. I am a firm believer in a more aggressive policy, based on a great deal of smashing—even against the best-length lobs—and as much variety as possible.

That does not imply that I believe in continual smashing with full force. There is no profit in putting every ounce of energy into a succession of strokes which have little, if any, chance of scoring outright. And a Badminton single is an affair so very strenuous that no one, however fit and active, can afford to waste energy. But a smash of moderate pace can be used, even against the most exemplary lobs, without any undue expenditure of energy, and is a fine weapon for keeping an attack going. A most effective sort of half-smash can be played from the very back of the court, just fast enough to bring the shuttlecock down sharply as it crosses the net. When a real opening presents itself, however, there should be no half-measures. Once in a way, in dealing with a short lob, a drop-shot—in place of the smash naturally expected—may be the most effective winning stroke. But in nine cases out of ten a full-powered smash is the right way to finish the rally, and a capable player must be prepared, while hitting with all his strength, to place within an inch or two of the spot aimed at. A Badminton court is a small area ; and it is only rarely—against an opponent with a sound defence—that there will be more than a very narrow space into which to place an unreturnable shot. A few wasted openings—however slight those openings may be—will make all the difference in the result of a close match. The ability to kill with certainty, whenever a bare opening occurs, is to my mind the greatest asset of all in a single.

However aggressive may be a player's methods, he cannot always attack. I hold firmly, nevertheless, to the opinion that when compelled to defend one should defend in such a way as to be always aiming at seizing the attack directly it becomes possible. Therefore, in returning smashes, for example, I would prefer to counter them, in general, by low-angled strokes rather than by deep lobs ; though, of course, not so persistently as to make these tactics stereotyped. Variety, as I have said already, is one of the main ingredients of attacking play ; and it is equally important in countering attack. Half a dozen consecutive defensive lobs may be a very effective variant to methods in the main quite different ; but only, in my theory of tactics at any rate, as a variant, not as a constant principle.

The more a player varies his tactics, the more difficult he makes it for his opponent to use that valuable, but easily abused, weapon anticipation. In Badminton, anticipation is very much a double-edged tool ; because a skilful player can change the nature of his stroke so surely at the very last moment, that the opponent who has gambled on some particular event is very likely to be left lamenting. I do not mean that anticipation should be neglected. Discreetly used, it is one of the hallmarks of a competent player ; but in a single, far more than in a double, it needs to be kept strictly within bounds. A player should be quick to realize what his opponent is most likely to do ; and, acting on that assumption, should move as far as he can without compromising himself, to the appropriate part of the court. But not, except in very rare cases, to the extent of gambling on it. At the precise moment when his opponent strikes, he should check his anticipatory movement, thus retaining the ability to move at once in some other direction should his forecast prove incorrect. By observing this precaution he will, admittedly, rob himself of an occasional opening ; but by neglecting it he will, against any opponent with a supple wrist and quick brain, lose far more than he gains.

In manœuvring for an opening, position in court is naturally very important. As a general rule, the most favourable base for operations is a point near the centre of the court. Obviously, the player will be driven away from this base with practically every stroke; but he must normally return to it as quickly as he can. With this end in view, he should not, if he can help it, play a stroke while still moving away from his base. Time permitting, he should be already poised for his return journey—perhaps even already started on it—before making his shot. While striving to keep his own position, all his efforts will be directed to forcing his opponent away from his. In this connection it must be remembered that the point farthest from a player is by no means necessarily the point most difficult for him to reach. A Badminton court is so small that an active man, moving in a direction for which he is prepared, can cover the necessary ground in next to no time. The whole art of placing is to make him turn in the most awkward direction.

Although, in the main, a point near the centre of the court is the most natural base, this should be modified a little according to the direction of the player's last stroke. He should edge slightly, but only slightly, towards the side to which he has played, as this tends to lessen the angle of danger in his opponent's return. This angle of danger is of supreme importance when playing anything but a purely defensive time-saving lob from near a side-line. In such a case it is most dangerous to try a quick cross-court stroke if there is any chance of the opponent reaching it before the striker can get back to mid-court, as the whole of the far side-line will be undefended.

While no one can afford to waste energy in a single, it is very false economy to spare it when it can be usefully employed. There are innumerable situations where a player, moving comparatively slowly, can reach the shuttlecock in time to take it after a fashion, but with his feet perhaps awkwardly placed, and with consequent loss of control, power and choice of stroke. In such cases it will pay him far better to make the extra effort required to bring him quickly into position, in time to play comfortably whatever stroke he prefers—possibly even to intercept the shuttlecock before it reaches an awkward spot. This is particularly true when dealing with a shot which, if allowed to complete its full course, will necessitate playing from the back left-hand corner. Whenever possible, these shots should be intercepted in mid-flight. Not so much because of any special danger in taking them later—no properly equipped player need fear that—but because the position is tactically disadvantageous. When interception is not possible—or at least when it is not possible to play the stroke quite high—it is usually best to allow the shuttlecock to fall very near the ground before hitting it. A shuttlecock travels slowly towards the end of its flight, and the extra time gained by letting it drop almost to the floor can be profitably utilized for getting into better position; while the sweep of the arm when hitting upwards from near the floor has greater potential power than when exerted at a higher level.

The benefit of getting to the shuttlecock quickly, in order to have the fullest option in the choice of one's own stroke, is very marked when countering drop-shots. A drop-shot taken late often permits very little option in reply; the choice is apt to lie between a safety lob and a more or less dangerous return drop-shot. Taken near the tape, however, it allows the striker a wealth of choice—straight or cross-court drop, a drive in any direction, or an attacking lob. Some of the most deceptive strokes in the game can be played from this position; but an inch or two in the height at which they are taken makes all the difference.

This habit of getting into position for a stroke as early as possible is, I believe, one of the most important principles in tactics. The point, however, is to be there in time to have a wide option in the choice of a stroke. It by no means follows that it is always best to play the stroke directly one is in position. Delaying it slightly may be a very effective move against an opponent who is apt to gamble on anticipation; he may be lured into committing himself to some unwise movement during the momentary pause, and so be caught on the wrong foot. But the more time one has to spare in such a manœuvre, the more likely is it to be successful.

In working for an opening, drop-shots are of great value and should be freely used. But it should be remembered that, except in comparatively rare cases, their function is to seek to open the court for a winning stroke rather than to be, in themselves, winners. Unless hopelessly out of position, or caught on the wrong foot, an active player can reach practically any drop-shot; the idea usually is just to land him in some difficulty. Consequently it is seldom worth while to play a drop-shot so closely as to risk an error. I am not advocating a wide

Plates 6—7

HIGH BACKHAND LOB (R. C. F. NICHOLS). FINISH OF SMASH (R. M. WHITE).

THE ARM IS AT FULL STRETCH AT THE MOMENT OF IMPACT AND THE WEIGHT OF THE BODY HAS BEEN THROWN FORWARD

margin of safety. Badminton is a game in which an almost uncanny measure of accuracy is possible ; and, to be effective, drop-shots should be cut very fine. All I mean is that super-accuracy should not be aimed at unless there is some special need for it. It is not worth taking a risk unless the chance of scoring outright is proportionately good and not to be attained *without* risk. Where there is a reasonable chance of scoring outright with a drop-shot, a good player should be able to place the stroke closely enough for the purpose with almost unfailing certainty. When playing drop-shots against an opponent waiting at the net, the utmost accuracy is, of course, essential ; and there are plenty of occasions when a player is in such an awkward hole that some desperately daring stroke is his best resource. But purposeless risk is always to be avoided ; and to cut a stroke unnecessarily fine simply for the pleasure of doing so is sheer folly. Yet one sees innumerable drop-shots come to grief, even among experts, for no better reason.

A clever player will naturally order his tactics to some extent according to the style of his opponent. But it is easy, and a sad error, to carry this idea too far. Against a player with a very powerful smash, for example, it is only common sense to restrict, as far as may be, his opportunities for its use. But it is a very common mistake to become more or less hypnotized by the fear of some particular danger ; and, in going too far out of one's way to avoid it, to fall into greater difficulties. In a general way, it is far more dangerous to play a stroke unsuited to the conditions of the moment than to do something more natural, even though it may permit the opponent the use of his favourite weapon. A much better plan for countering such a pet stroke is to make its use as dangerous as possible. Against the player with a deadly smash, for instance, one should try to attack that smash ; stepping forward to it and meeting it at the earliest possible point in its flight, with the idea of returning it before the striker can recover his balance ; or, when there is not time for that, at least taking it high enough to drive it in some form of counter-attack. To meet a favourite form of attack by purely defensive measures is, I am sure, a fatal mistake, except for a player of superlative defensive powers. It allows the aggressor so much scope in grading the intensity of his attack, and permits him to call the tune all the time. But if it can be impressed on him that even his best attacking strokes may come back in the shape of counter-attack, the effect will be most salutary.

Conversely, it is very easy to fall into the error of concentrating too directly on any weakness in the opponent's make-up. The natural tendency of a player conscious of some particular weakness is to cover it as far as possible. Attacking it continually simply makes it easy for him to guard it. Much more effective is the plan of drawing the defence away from the weak spot by attacking in some other direction and then playing on to the real target. Almost every player below the first class is relatively weak at defending from the backhand corner of the base-line; advantage can most readily be taken of this weakness by drawing him first to some point on his forehand side-line not far from the net and then placing deeply to the other wing.

General practice in singles favours the almost exclusive use of the high service. This is, in the main, a sound principle; but I think most players carry it too far. It is true that, with the full length of the court to serve into as compared with the shorter length available in doubles, the receiver's chance of killing outright a really good-length service is comparatively small, even allowing for the width of court the server has to defend single-handed. On the other hand, by reason of this extra available length, the receiver must stand farther back while waiting for the service than he would in doubles; and so leaves a greater margin of safety for a short service. It is very seldom indeed that a reasonably good short service can be rushed in a single; only, in fact, when the receiver has had reason to expect it and has gambled on his intuition. The only real danger inherent to short services in a single—unless they be used in excess—lies in the fact that the receiver may, by a very well-judged drop-shot, secure a favourable attacking position. This danger is more than counterbalanced by the advantage derived from using short services sufficiently often to keep the opponent guessing and prevent him waiting as far back in court as he might otherwise do. The deep service should, however, certainly be the more frequent method of opening the rally.

CHAPTER SIX

DOUBLES

EXCEPT in the mixed variety, which will be considered separately, the formation usually adopted in doubles is one in which the partners work more or less side by side. This is certainly the best formation for a pair of men or a pair of women, except in rare cases where the special talents of a player call for other methods; or where there is a marked discrepancy of strength between the partners.

The phrase 'side by side' must not, however, be taken too literally. Intelligently practised, the formation is in a constant state of flux. As a basic principle, each partner is normally responsible for covering his own half of the court; but each must be constantly in readiness to cross either in front of or behind the other in response to any special requirement of the moment. This, for purposes of either attack or defence. Badminton is a game in which there is much scope for opportunism; and many an ace is scored (or saved) by the player quick to seize an opening (or guard a danger) outside his normal sphere, but for which he is momentarily better placed than his partner. This sort of thing depends largely on anticipation, which can be exercised much more freely in doubles than in singles; since, where there is a proper understanding between the partners, the one who gambles on an opening can rely on the other to save the situation—if things go wrong—by covering any part of the gambler's court which has been left unguarded.

Even when there is no special chance to be snapped up, it is often advisable for a player who has been drawn to the net to remain there for a time, guarding the whole width of the net while his partner becomes responsible for the entire back portion of the court. No precise rules can be laid down for such action. It must depend on the circumstances of the moment. The point is that the partners must be ready to work in and out systematically, the one who abandons his normal position for any purpose being assured that the other will automatically cover any part of the court exposed by his action.

When one player is smashing from far back in court, the partner should always edge forward, ready to deal with any return near the net. Not only may he snap up a chance of scoring, but he can also save his partner any trouble consequent on a short quick return before he has fully recovered his balance. The player smashing can go for his stroke much more wholeheartedly if assured that a momentary loss of mobility will not matter.

When smashing from farther forward in court, however, it is usually better for the player to follow up his own stroke himself. Knowing exactly where he means to place his smash, he will be better able to gauge the most likely angle of return ; while the impetus natural to his stroke can be used to carry him forward. In this case, a really good lob in return may trouble him, so his partner must be prepared to guard him against that instead of against a drop-shot.

When the server opens the rally with a short service, it is often useful for him to follow it up, so as to take any return in the nature of a drop-shot, his partner naturally falling back to balance matters. This is one of the tactical problems on which there is no uniformity of practice among the experts ; and it is very essential that the partners should have a clear understanding as to the method they adopt.

A detail of combination in which even quite strong pairs are often at fault concerns the duty of taking cross-court shots which, passing first just within range of one player, would, if not intercepted, finish in his partner's zone. In such cases, I think the player across whom the shuttlecock passes should take it whenever he is in position to make anything in the nature of an attacking stroke ; but if reduced to defence, he should leave the shot to his partner, who will have more time to deal with it safely.

Even more definitely than in singles, tactics in doubles should be based on severity. In a single, sufficiently clever and varied placing may, though lacking in severity, be quite an efficient form of attack. In doubles, against opponents who back each other up intelligently, it is not enough. Clever placing is, of course, of immense value in working for an opening, and drop-shots should be freely used. But, almost without exception, when there is any opportunity for hitting hard that is the best course to adopt. Like all similar principles, however, this can easily be carried too far. A strong defensive pair, suitably placed, can put in some astounding work in the way of returning a series of smashes, however powerful. But in doing so, they are apt to plant themselves rather firmly on their feet, sacrificing, to some slight extent, the ability of starting quickly forward. Thus entrenched, it may prove almost impossible to beat down their defence by sheer battering. But here, a properly disguised drop-shot, breaking the sequence of smashes, may be far more effective than undiluted force, upsetting for a moment, if nothing more, the solidity of the defensive position. Even an alteration in the pace of the smashes may produce good results. This is simply another example of the necessity, always present in Badminton, of trying to surprise the opponent. The importance of variety cannot be stressed too emphatically. But, in the main, it is severity which finishes the rallies.

While the partners may be about equal in general strength, they are quite likely to be widely dissimilar in style, and each may have special ability in some particular direction. Anything of this nature should influence their tactics. Obviously, for example, the player with the better smash should be left the greater share of overhead work. What is not so evident is that this principle is at least as important in defence. Anyone particularly good at returning smashes may do a great deal of lobbing with impunity as far as he himself is concerned. But unless his partner has an equal talent in the same direction, persistent lobbing will be very dangerous; since the player with the weaker defence will be the mark of attack whenever a lob of at all inferior length invites punishment.

Mixed doubles differ fundamentally from other varieties because here, apart from any question of skill, the man will normally be more active and a harder hitter than his partner. That is the idea on which the back-and-front formation, so prevalent in mixed doubles, is based. In this formation, the respective duties of the partners are quite distinct, each having a definite zone to guard. The lady deals with all drop-shots, and with certain other shots which she can intercept without retreating from her line of action, which should be somewhere in the neighbourhood of the short service-line. The man takes everything else. This formation is adopted as early as practicable in each rally.

When the lady is serving, the required positions can be taken up at once, as she can serve from a point near the junction of the centre and short service-lines. She should deliver a short service far more often than not, so as to give the opposition as few openings as possible for attack. But she must introduce sufficient variety to keep the receiver in a state of uncertainty ; otherwise, even her most accurate short services may be rushed too frequently.

Similarly, when the lady is being served to, she should go to the net directly she has played her stroke. When receiving a low service she should take it as early as she can, even though it be too good to be rushed, so as to avoid as far as possible having to play an upward stroke. When taking a high service, she should smash practically always, even though not in position to do so with any real severity. By playing a drop-shot in such a case she invites another one, very close to the net, in return, and this is almost certain to be a good way below the level of the tape before she can reach it, so that she will be forced to hit upwards ; and the more accurate her own drop-shot has been, the more likely is the return to put her on the defensive. By choosing even a half-smash of very moderate pace instead of the drop-shot she can avoid much of this danger ; for though the reply may still be a drop-shot it will come back at quite a different angle, and one not nearly so likely to throw her on the defensive. This point is, in my opinion, of much greater importance than is generally realized. In any exchange of close drop-shots, the player who is first at the net starts with an advantage.

When the man is serving or receiving service, the immediate adoption of the back-and-front position is not so simple ; and my personal opinion—though some of the best players disagree —is that it is better to delay it for one stroke. With his partner waiting back for the first return, the man has much greater freedom in his choice of service ; not only in the type of service itself, but in the position from which he delivers it. Again, when the man is being served to, he will be better able to deal effectively with short services if secure in the knowledge that, should he rush one and fail to kill it, he will not be in the hopeless position of having to get back from within a few inches of the net to defend the whole of his own base-line. That, at least, is my view. Some think it better for the lady to go to the net at once, irrespective of special circumstances. It is one of the points individual pairs must decide for themselves, and may turn, to a considerable extent, on whether or no the man is of more than average agility, and so capable of feats of retrieving which would be beyond another's powers. When the man has to return a high service, his partner should, of course, go forward at once. But his opponents will naturally seek to draw him from his base as often as possible; so will give him as many short services as they consider consistent with prudence.

Once the back-and-front formation has been secured, it should not be abandoned except under the most exceptional circumstances. Even when the man is very hard pressed in defence, any attempt by his partner to drop back to his assistance will probably do more harm than good.

The first duty of the net-player is to hit down, and hit down *sharply*, whenever possible. She must be alert to seize the most fleeting opening and deal with it decisively. The actual chances which come her way will frequently allow only the smallest margin of error. But she must go for them confidently; and, whenever there is a chance of scoring outright, it is better for her to take a legitimate risk than to play a tentative stroke which will simply start the rally all over again. Most of her chances of killing will be only a few inches above the tape, so must be dealt with by a flick of the wrist only, but need not be any the less decisive on that account. When she cannot hit down she must at least do all she can to avoid hitting up, except on the rare occasions when a comparatively low lob may be a means of attack.

There are many occasions when it is difficult for the net-player to decide whether to intercept a shot or leave it to her partner; but she must make her decision and act on it instantaneously. This applies particularly to straight shots down the side-lines. When in doubt, it is nearly always best for her to leave such a shot—for two reasons. First, because this doubtful shot is just the one to draw her momentarily out of position and leave the far corner of the net exposed; and in the second place because, by intercepting a shot which her partner is preparing to take himself, she will very likely leave him stranded on the wrong foot. The man in a back-and-front combination has a great deal of ground to cover, and must be very quick in getting off the mark. It is far easier for him to complete his run, himself playing a stroke the nature of which he designs and for the reply to which he is consequently prepared, than to check himself half-way through his movement and prepare for the reply to his partner's stroke, which is, quite possibly, not the one best suited to his own position in court.

Leaving the shuttlecock when in doubt calls for a lot of self-restraint from the net-player, and may result in her going for a considerable period without playing a stroke at all. But throughout such a period of apparent inactivity she can be helping her partner enormously by shifting her own position in accordance with the direction of his strokes, so as to block as far as possible the angle of any aggressive reply open to the opponents. For instance, when her partner is smashing straight down a line, the reply he has most to fear is a quick cross-court drive. She should, therefore, take position where she has the best chance of intercepting such a drive, without of course sacrificing her ability to guard the full width of the net. Interception of this kind calls for extraordinarily quick action, and is one of the most difficult of the net-player's duties. But when efficiently performed it can be very profitable, everything happening so quickly that the pace of the opponent's drive is turned to his own disadvantage. As a rough guide it may be laid down that the net-player should leave any shot which she would have to play with the shuttlecock farther than herself from the net. But should she start to take such a shot, it is usually better for her to go on with it than to draw back at the last moment, when her partner will probably have checked his own movement in accord with her apparent intention. Vacillation almost always turns out worse than a badly judged action carried through with determination.

The man's tactics vary a good deal according to the formation adopted by his opponents. Against a side-by-side pair he can make a liberal use of drop-shots, with the idea of forcing his opponents either to hit up to him or to take on his partner at an exchange of drop-shots, where she starts with the advantage of being already in position. He must, of course, smash fiercely when he has a chance for effective attack, but should not waste energy in this way ; and his efforts in working for an opening should be directed rather towards calling the tune than making the pace too fast. He must also be very alert to notice if either of the opponents is edging forward to punish his drop-shots. A judicious proportion of good-length lobs provide the best counter to such a movement. Lobbing should not, however, be resorted to without some definite purpose, such as that. Too much of it is a very grave mistake; for the back-and-front formation is essentially an attacking one.

Against another back-and-front pair, the back player's opportunities for dropping are naturally somewhat restricted. Here, the rallies constantly resolve into a duel between the two men, with their partners not only ready to chip in at the first opportunity, but also closing, as far as they can, the most likely avenue of attack by the other side. Should one of the men, however, find himself constantly out-manœuvred, or beaten by superior pace, he must try to give the game a different turn by attacking the opposing net-player, at whatever risk. Straight drives down the line—some deep, some comparatively short—play a great part in the duels between the two men. But a cross-court drive, though far more dangerous because of the extra risk of interception, is particularly effective at the right moment.

The short, straight shot down either line—just too deep to come properly within the province of the net-player—is one of the most useful weapons against back-and-front tactics. It may tempt the net-player to take a shot she ought to leave; or it draws the man away from his natural base to a position where he has little chance of doing anything aggressive. Many players, however, seem to forget that its main purpose is to open up the back of the court; the man, having been drawn forward, should usually be forced back again by a drive or an attacking lob. A continuous stream of half-court strokes defeat their own purpose, the opposing man simply working from a comparatively forward base, and having a much easier time than if kept right back.

So much for the strict back-and-front formation. Some of the best pairs in mixed doubles modify it very considerably. In this system, the lady is in no hurry to get to the net, sharing much of the general work with her partner, especially in defence. When he gets a good opening for attack, however, she takes position at the net and usually remains there until the end of the rally; unless her partner is forced back on to the defensive, in which case she may drop back again to his assistance. This can be a very effective form of combination. It combines most of the advantages of the back-and-front game in attack with greater solidity in defence, while saving the man from too continuous a strain on his energy. But it is very difficult to reach the same certainty of combination as in the true back-

and-front game and the opponents have a good deal more latitude in developing their own tactics. It is only effective, too, when the lady is a really first-rate all-round player. A few pairs even play a side-by-side game on the lines of a man's double. But this cannot possibly be successful unless the lady has altogether exceptional powers of defence.

CHAPTER
SEVEN

THE LAWS OF BADMINTON

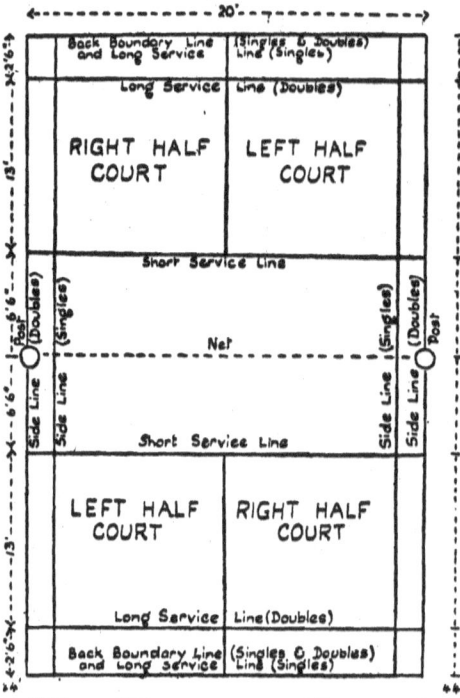

Fig. A.

(1) The posts shall be placed on the side boundary lines of the court.

(2) Where it is not possible for the posts to be placed on the side boundary lines, some method must be employed for indicating the position of the side boundary line where it passes under the net, (e.g.) by the side of a thin post or by a strip of material not less than 2 inches in width fixed to the side boundary line and rising vertically to the net cord.

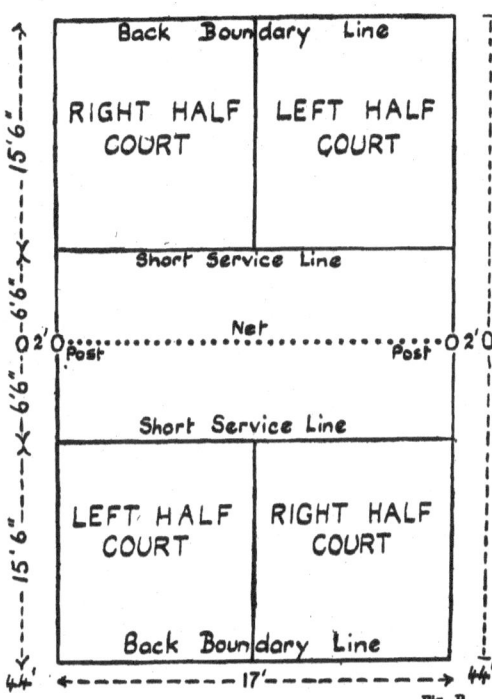

Fig. B.

Where space does not permit of the marking out of a full-size court in accordance with Law No. 1, a court may be marked out for singles play only, and, in that case, the provisions of footnotes (1) and (2) to Figure A shall apply to such court. The back boundary lines become the long service lines.

CHAPTER SEVEN

THE LAWS OF BADMINTON

THE COURTS

1. The Court shall be laid out as in the preceding Fig. A, and defined by white or black lines 1½ inches wide.

Note.—Where space does not permit of the marking out of a full-size court referred to above, a court may be marked out for singles play only as shown in Fig. B.

2. The net shall be made of fine tanned cord of ¾ of an inch mesh, and shall be firmly stretched from post to post, and sufficiently long, when so stretched, to extend to the side boundary lines, and be 2 feet 6 inches in depth. The top of the net shall be 5 feet in height at the centre, and 5 feet 1 inch at the posts, and shall be edged with a 3-inch white tape doubled and supported by a cord run through the tape and strained over and flush with the top of the posts.

3. The posts shall be 5 feet 1 inch in height and shall be sufficiently firm to keep the net strained as above.

4. The shuttles shall weigh from 73 to 85 grains, and shall have from 14 to 16 feathers fixed in a cork 1 inch to 1⅛ inch in diameter. The feathers shall be from 2½ to 2¾ inches in length, shall have from 2⅜ to 2½ inches spread at the top, and shall be firmly fastened and cemented at a height of about 1 inch above the cork, with thread.

Note.—A shuttlecock shall be deemed to be of correct pace if, when a player of average strength strikes it with a full underhand stroke with a reasonably tightly strung racket from a spot immediately above one back boundary line in a line parallel to the side lines, and at an upward angle of approximately 45 degrees, it falls not less than 1 foot and not more than 2 feet 6 inches short of the back boundary line.

THE FOUR-HANDED OR DOUBLE GAME

5. The game is played by two players a side.

6. THE CHOICE OF COURTS. The side winning the toss shall have first choice of—
 (a) Serving first;
 (b) Not serving first;
 (c) Ends.

The side losing the toss shall then have choice of any alternative remaining. The side winning a game shall always serve first in the next game, but in doubles either of the winners may continue serving and either of the losers may receive the service.

7. The four-handed game consists of 15 or 21 aces, as may be arranged. Provided that in a game of 15 aces, when the score is 13 all, the side which first reached 13 has the option of 'setting' the game to 5, and that when the score is 14 all the side which first reached 14 has the option of 'setting' the game to 3. After a game has been 'set' the score is called 'love all', and the side which first scores 5 or 3 aces, according as the game has been 'set' at 13 or 14 all, wins the game. In either case the claim to 'set' the game must be made before the next service is delivered after the score has reached 13 all or 14 all. Provided also that in a game of 21 aces the same method of scoring be adopted, substituting 19 and 20 for 13 and 14.

Note.—'Setting' is not permitted in handicap games.

THE LAWS OF BADMINTON

8. A rubber is the best of three games. The players shall change ends at the commencement of the second game, and also of the third game, if a third game is necessary to decide the rubber. In the third game the players shall also change ends, when the leading score reaches 8, in a game of 15 aces, at 6, in a game of 11 aces, or 11 in a game of 21 aces, or in handicap games, when either side has scored half the total number of aces required to win the game (the next highest number being taken in case of fractions). In matches decided by a single game the players shall change ends as provided above for the third game of a rubber.

FAULTS

9. A fault made by either player of the side which is 'in' puts the server out; if made by a player whose side is 'out', it counts an ace to the 'in' side.

10. It is a fault—
    (a) If the service is overhand. (A service shall be deemed to be overhand, within the meaning of this law, if the shuttle at the instant of being struck be higher than the server's waist, or if any part of the head of the racket, at the instant of striking the shuttle, is higher than the server's hand holding the racket.)
    (b) If, in serving, the shuttle falls into the wrong half court (i.e. into the one not diagonally opposite to the server), or falls short of the short service-line, or beyond the long service-line, or outside the side boundary lines of the half court into which service is in order.
    (c) If the server's feet are not in the half-court from which service is at the time being in order, or if the feet of the player taking the service are not in the half court into which service is at the time being in order (vide Law 15) until the service is delivered.
    Note (1).—A 'service' is delivered as soon as the shuttle is struck by the server's racket.
    Note (2).—A foot on the line is out of court.
    (d) If during the service the server or his partner makes, in the opinion of the umpire, preliminary feints, or otherwise intentionally baulks his opponent.
    (e) If, either in service or play, the shuttle falls outside the boundaries, or passes through or under the net, or fails to pass the net, or touches the roof or side walls, or the person or dress of any player.
    Note.—A shuttle falling on any line is held to have fallen in the court or half court of which such line is a boundary.
    (f) If the shuttle 'in play' be struck before it crosses to the striker's side of the net. The striker may, however, follow the shuttle over the net with his racket.
    Note.—A shuttle is 'in play' from the time it is hit by the racket of the server until it touches the ground, or the person, or dress of any player, or until a fault or let occurs (vide Knotty Points (f)).
    (g) If, when the shuttle is 'in play', a player touch the net or its supports with racket, person, or dress.
    (h) If the shuttle be hit twice in succession by the same player, or be hit by a player and his partner successively, or if the shuttle be not distinctly hit.
    (i) If a player obstructs his opponents.
    (k) If Rule 15 be transgressed.

THE PLAY

11. It having been decided which side is to have the first service, the player in the right-hand half-court of that side commences the game by serving to the player in the opposite right-hand half-court. If the latter player returns the shuttle before it touches the ground, it is to be returned by one of the 'in' side, and then returned by one of the 'out' side, and so on, till a fault is made or the shuttle ceases to be 'in play'. If a fault is made by the 'in' side, the servers' hand is out, and as the side beginning a game has only one hand in its first innings (vide Law 14), the player in the right-hand opposite half court now becomes the server; but if the service is not returned, or the fault is made by the 'out' side, the 'in' side scores an ace. The 'in' side players then change from one half-court to the other, the server now being in the left-hand half court and serving to the player in the opposite left-hand half court.

D

So long as a side remains 'in', service is delivered alternately from each half court into the one diagonally opposite, the change being made by the 'in' side when, and only when, an ace is added to its score. The first service of a side in each innings shall be made from the right-hand half court. After the service is delivered, the server and the player served to may take up any positions they choose on their side of the net, irrespective of any boundary lines.

GENERAL RULES

12. The player served to may alone take the service and no player may take two consecutive services in the same game.

13. The server may not serve till his opponent is ready, but if a return of the service be attempted the latter shall be deemed to be ready.

14. The side beginning a game has only one hand in its first innings. In all subsequent innings each partner on each side has a hand, the partners serving consecutively.

15. The server and the player served to must stand within the limits of their respective half courts (as bounded by the short and long service, the central, and side lines), and some part of both feet of these players must remain in contact with the ground until the service is delivered.—*Vide Notes to Law* 10 (c), *supra*.

16. It is a 'Let' if the shuttle touches the net in service, provided the service be otherwise good, but if in play it does not invalidate the stroke. It is a good return if the shuttle having passed outside either post drop on or within any of the boundary lines of the opposite court. A 'Let' may also be given by the umpire for any unforeseen or accidental hindrance.

17. If a player serves out of his turn, or from the wrong half court (owing to a mistake as to the half court from which service is at the time being in order), and wins the ace, it shall be a 'Let', provided such 'Let' be claimed or allowed before the next succeeding service is delivered.

18. If a player standing in his wrong half court takes the service, and his side wins the rally, it shall be a 'Let' provided that such 'Let' be claimed or allowed before the next succeeding service is delivered.

Note.—Should a player inadvertently change sides when he ought not to, and the mistake not be discovered until after the next service has been delivered, the mistake shall stand and a 'Let' cannot be claimed or allowed.

19. It shall be the duty of the umpire to call 'fault' or 'let', should either occur, without appeal being made by the players, and to give his decision on any appeal regarding a point in dispute, if made before the next service; and also to appoint linesmen if necessary. In matches where umpires are appointed, their decision shall be final, but where a referee is appointed, an appeal shall lie to him from the decision of an umpire on questions of law only.

THE TWO-HANDED OR SINGLE GAME

20. In games of one player on each side, the above rules hold good, except that—

(a) The players shall serve from and receive service in the right-hand half courts only when the server's score is 0, or when he has scored an even number of aces in the game, the service being delivered from and received in the left-hand half courts when the server has scored an odd number of aces.

(b) Both players shall change half courts after each ace has been scored, and consecutive services shall be received by the same player.

(c) In Ladies' Singles matches the game shall consist of 11 aces. Provided that when the score is 9 all the side which first reaches 9 has the option of 'setting' the game to 5, and when the score is 10 all the side which first reached 10 may 'set' the game to 3.

N.B.—The courts for the Single Game are laid out as provided in Figure B, and the notes thereto appended.

THE LAWS OF BADMINTON

KNOTTY POINTS

Addenda to the Laws of the Game approved by the International Federation.

(a) If the server in attempting to serve misses the shuttle altogether, it does not count as a fault; but if the shuttle be touched, no matter how slightly, by the racket, a service is thereby delivered, and the rules governing the service at once apply.

(b) If A is serving to B and the shuttle strikes or is struck by B's partner, even if he is standing outside the court, A scores an ace.

(c) A player who strikes the shuttle in play (unless he thereby makes a good return), or is struck by it, loses the stroke, no matter whether he is standing within the boundaries of the court or outside them.

(d) If in service the shuttle strikes the top of the net, and is then struck by the player served to, it is assumed that the shuttle would have fallen into the proper court. It is thus a 'Let' under Law 16, and a fault cannot be claimed.

(e) If in service, or during a rally, a shuttle after passing over the net, is caught in or on the net, it shall be a 'let'.

(f) If during a rally, the shuttle strikes the net and remains suspended there, or strikes the net and falls thence to the ground on the striker's side of the net, or hits the ground outside the court and an opponent *then* touches the net with his racket or person, there is no penalty, as the shuttle is not then in play.—*Vide Note to Law* 10 (f).

(g) The word 'player' applies to all those taking part in a game from the moment the shuttle is struck by the server.

(h) If a player has a chance of smashing when quite near the net, his opponent must not put up his racket near the net on the chance of the shuttlecock rebounding from it. This action shall be taken to be obstruction within the meaning of Law 10 (i).
A player may, however, hold up his racket to protect his face from being hit if he does not thereby baulk his opponent.

(i) Law 10 (c) applies only to the server and to the player taking the service. The respective partners may take up any position, provided they do not unsight or otherwise obstruct their opponents.

HINTS TO UMPIRES

BEFORE PLAY COMMENCES:
See that the net is the correct height.
If there are linesmen, see that they understand their duties and are placed where you can see them.
If the rules of the tournament give you control over the shuttles, have three or four tested shuttles ready, and do not sanction a change without good reason.

SERVICE:
Watch that the shuttle when struck is not above the server's waist.
NOTE.—It is almost impossible to judge this from a chair, and it is therefore well to delegate this duty to a linesman—on either side if possible.
Watch for a 'let'.
Watch the fall of the shuttle if it be not taken.
Watch that the striker-out does not leave his court before the service is delivered.

PLAY:
Keep your eye on the shuttle.
Remember that a player who strikes a shuttle before it passes the net, or who, before the shuttle is dead, touches the net or its supports with racket, person or clothes, loses the point.
Great care is necessary to avoid mistakes as to the number of hands in.
When a score at which setting is permissible is reached, ask the player who first reached that score whether he wishes to set.
See that the players change sides at the proper score in the third game.

FOUL STROKES:
It is often a matter of considerable difficulty to decide whether a fault has been committed

under Law 10 (*h*), In every case in which the umpire feels any doubt in this respect, he should give the benefit to the striker ; only penalizing a stroke when he is certain that Law 10 (*h*) has been contravened.

N.B.—Where a game is played without an umpire, it must of course be left to the good sense of the players to carry out the intention of Law 10 (*h*) ; but if players will keep in mind the Hints to Umpires quoted above, the proper interpretation of the Law should not be difficult.

GENERAL :

Remember that it is your opinion that is to lead you to a decision, not that of the players, still less that of the spectators.

If you cannot give a decision do not be afraid to say so ; in such a case, accept the opinion of the players if they are agreed, otherwise you must give a let.

Give your decisions as promptly as possible, but remember that over-anxiety to be smart may lead you into error.

Call the score clearly at the end of each rally, and loudly enough to be heard by spectators as well as players.

Where a linesman is appointed, his decision on all points relative to the line is absolutely final.

On the conclusion of a match take the score to the referee at once.

HALL SUITABLE FOR BADMINTON

The following are the main requisites in a Hall suitable for one or more Courts.

HEIGHT. Not less than 25 feet over the middle of the Court.

SPACE ROUND COURT. Where there is only one Court, there should be at least 3 feet clear all round it. Where two courts lie side by side, they should be 4 feet apart.

BACKGROUND. This should be uniform in colour and of a darkish shade. Dull green is very suitable.

FLOOR. The colour of the floor should be dark rather than light. If stained, a dull stain should be used, not one that reflects light.

MARKING. The lines should be white : preferably painted with a mixture of very thin glue and whitewash.

POSTS. Those on a metal base screwed to the floor on the side line are most satisfactory, but where these cannot be used, posts with guy ropes or weighted bases will do well enough.

LIGHTING.

(1) *Daylight.*

This should come, if possible, from above, through skylights. In a Hall without skylights, light should only be admitted through windows at the sides of the Court ; any windows facing either end of the Court should be completely blocked out.

(2) *Artificial.*

(*a*) *Incandescent Gas.* Inverted mantles, with frosted or opalescent globes should be used. Good light is provided by a row of eight lamps (of about 80 c.p.) hanging on each side of the Court, about 12 or 13 feet above the floor and about 2 feet outside the side lines, the centre of the row of lamps being opposite the net post.

N.B.—The exact height above the floor at which the lamps give best results varies according to the particular features (height, colour of ceiling, &c.) of the Hall concerned, and can only be decided by experiment. The candle power required also varies to some extent.

(*b*) *Electric.* As with gas ; or with one naked light of about 750 c.p. at each side of the Court.

INDEX

Court, Plan of, 46, 47

Doubles, 38
Driving, 26
Drop Shots, 22

Footwork, 12

General Principles, 12
Grip, 14

Halls for Badminton, 52
History, 9

Knotty Points, 51

Laws, 48
Lobbing, 20

Mixed Doubles, 39

Pace, 16
Push-shots, 25

Returning Service, 30

Service, 28
Singles, 31
Smashing, 18
Striking, 15
Strokes, 18

Umpires, Hints to, 51

www.ingramcontent.com/pod-product-compliance
Lightning Source LLC
Chambersburg PA
CBHW021813220426
43662CB00006B/301